LIFE IN A
Grassland

by Laura Hamilton Waxman

BELLWETHER MEDIA • MINNEAPOLIS, MN

Note to Librarians, Teachers, and Parents:

Blastoff! Readers are carefully developed by literacy experts and combine standards-based content with developmentally appropriate text.

Level 1 provides the most support through repetition of high-frequency words, light text, predictable sentence patterns, and strong visual support.

Level 2 offers early readers a bit more challenge through varied simple sentences, increased text load, and less repetition of high-frequency words.

Level 3 advances early-fluent readers toward fluency through increased text and concept load, less reliance on visuals, longer sentences, and more literary language.

Level 4 builds reading stamina by providing more text per page, increased use of punctuation, greater variation in sentence patterns, and increasingly challenging vocabulary.

Level 5 encourages children to move from "learning to read" to "reading to learn" by providing even more text, varied writing styles, and less familiar topics.

Whichever book is right for your reader, Blastoff! Readers are the perfect books to build confidence and encourage a love of reading that will last a lifetime!

This edition first published in 2016 by Bellwether Media, Inc.

No part of this publication may be reproduced in whole or in part without written permission of the publisher. For information regarding permission, write to Bellwether Media, Inc., Attention: Permissions Department, 5357 Penn Avenue South, Minneapolis, MN 55419.

Library of Congress Cataloging-in-Publication Data

Waxman, Laura Hamilton, author.
  Life in a Grassland / by Laura Hamilton Waxman.
    pages cm. – (Blastoff! Readers. Biomes Alive!)
  Summary: "Simple text and full-color photography introduce beginning readers to life in a grassland. Developed by literacy experts for students in kindergarten through third grade"– Provided by publisher.
  Audience: Ages 5-8.
  Audience: K to grade 3.
  Includes bibliographical references and index.
  ISBN 978-1-62617-318-7 (hardcover : alk. paper)
  1. Grassland ecology–Juvenile literature. 2. Grassland animals–Juvenile literature. 3. Grasslands–Climatic factors–Juvenile literature. I. Title.
  QH541.5.P7W284 2016
  577.4–dc23
                                                 2015031528

Table of Contents

The Grassland Biome

African savannah

The grassland **biome** is on every **continent** except Antarctica. The Great Plains stretch down North America. The Pampas fill part of South America. Africa has the Serengeti.

4

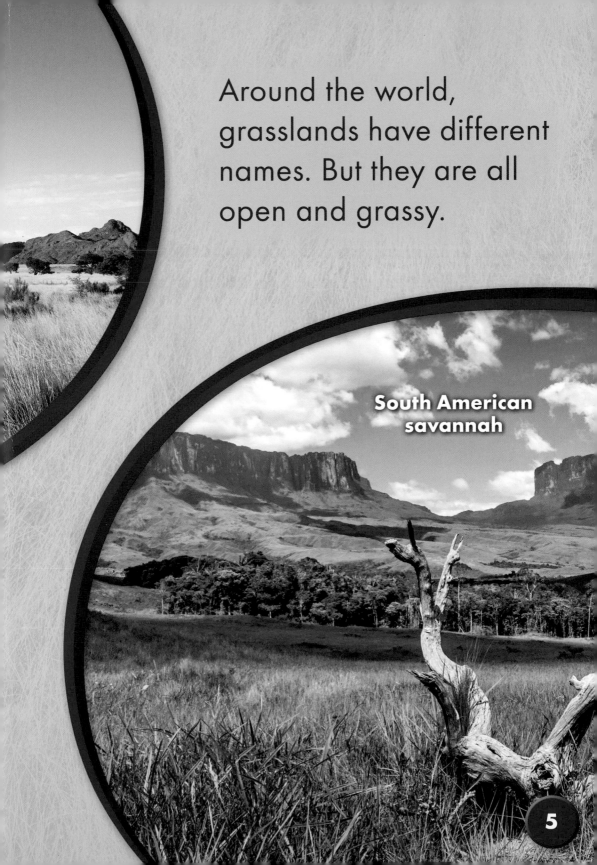

Around the world, grasslands have different names. But they are all open and grassy.

South American savannah

Tropical grasslands called savannahs are found close to the **equator**. Prairies, steppes, and other **temperate** grasslands lie farther north and south.

grasslands = ☐

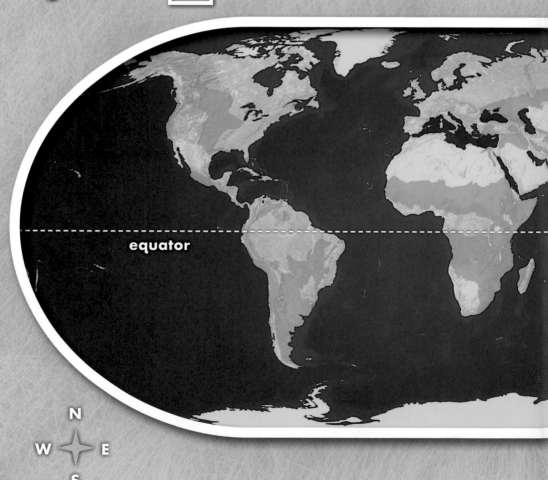

equator

N
W ✦ E
S

Grasslands are often between forests and deserts. They are drier than forests and wetter than deserts.

tropical grassland

temperate grassland

Gran Sabana, Venezuela

Tropical grasslands have a warm **climate**. Temperatures stay between 60 and 86 degrees Fahrenheit (16 and 30 degrees Celsius).

Bigger temperature changes happen in temperate grasslands. The summer heat can reach 100 degrees Fahrenheit (38 degrees Celsius). In winter, temperatures can drop well below **freezing**.

Great Plains, Colorado

Precipitation falls throughout the year in temperate grasslands. But tropical grasslands have a wet season and a dry season.

Serengeti,
Tanzania

savannah fire
in Kenya

Natural fires burn during the dry season. They burn down young trees and **shrubs**.

big bluestem
grass

The wettest grasslands have
tall grasses. They can be more
than 7 feet (2 meters) high!

Shorter grasses grow in the driest grasslands. They may be only 8 inches (20 centimeters) tall.

blue grama grass

Deep **roots** help many grassland plants reach water far underground. Narrow leaves soak in sunlight and keep in the water.

milkweed

candelabra
tree

A few kinds of trees grow in
tropical grasslands. Some store
a lot of water in their trunks. Thick
bark protects many from fires.

African lion

Grassland animals must survive out in the open. Many use **camouflage** to hide or hunt. Their colors, spots, or stripes help them blend in with the land.

Some small animals **burrow** underground. There, they stay cool and safe.

prairie dog

Large **grazers** feed on tough grasses and plant parts. These animals have strong, flat teeth for chewing.

American
bison

wildebeests

Many grazers **migrate** to wherever there is enough grass to eat. They stay safe by traveling together!

The Serengeti Plain

Location: Africa; Tanzania and Kenya

**Size of Serengeti National Park:
5,700 square miles (14,763 square kilometers)**

Temperature:

○ **Nighttime temperature:**
around 60 °F (16 °C)

○ **Daytime temperature:**
around 80 °F (27 °C)

**Precipitation: 41 inches (105 centimeters)
per year in the northwest; less than 21 inches
(55 centimeters) per year in the east**

SERENGETI PLAIN FOOD WEB

African lion

zebra

giraffe

savannah grasses

spotted hyena

acacia tree

Other important plants: pan dropseed grasses, red grasses, candelabra trees, whistling thorns, strangler figs, wild date palms

Other important animals: golden jackals, cheetahs, leopards, secretary birds, ostriches, elephants, rhinos, wildebeests, gazelles, puff adders

Glossary

biome—a nature community defined by its climate, land features, and living things

burrow—to make a hole or tunnel underground

camouflage—a way of using color to blend in with surroundings

climate—the specific weather conditions for an area

continent—one of the seven main land areas on Earth; the continents are Africa, Antarctica, Asia, Australia, Europe, North America, and South America.

equator—the imaginary line that divides Earth into northern and southern halves

freezing—32 degrees Fahrenheit (0 degrees Celsius); the temperature at which water freezes into ice.

grazers—animals that feed, or graze, on grasses

migrate—to travel from one place to another, often with the seasons

precipitation—water that falls to the earth from the sky

roots—the underground parts of a plant; roots hold a plant in place and take in water.

shrubs—short, woody plants

temperate—mild; not too hot or too cold.

tropical—relating to the tropics, a hot region near the equator

To Learn More

AT THE LIBRARY
Callery, Sean. *Grassland*. New York, N.Y.:
Kingfisher, 2011.

Duke, Shirley. *Seasons of the Grassland Biome*. Vero
Beach, Fla.: Rourke Educational Media, 2013.

Royston, Angela. *Grassland Food Chains*. Chicago,
Ill.: Heinemann Library, 2015.

ON THE WEB
Learning more about grasslands
is as easy as 1, 2, 3.

1. Go to www.factsurfer.com.

2. Enter "grasslands" into the search box.

3. Click the "Surf" button and you will see a
   list of related web sites.

With factsurfer.com, finding more
information is just a click away.

Index

The images in this book are reproduced through the courtesy of: Paul Reeves Photography, front cover (hawk); Dan Kaplan, front cover (pronghorn); biletskiy, front cover (background); JaySi, p. 4; Lukas Uher, p. 5; Vidu Gunaratna, p. 7 (top); Zack Frank, p. 7 (bottom); Vadim Petrakov, p. 8; marekuliasz, p. 9; Oleg Znamenskiy, p. 10; Byelikova Oksana, p. 11; Mike Grandmaison/ Corbis, p. 12; SharonFoelz, p. 13; Weldon Schloneger, p. 14; Papa Bravo, p. 15; Tabby Mittins, p. 16; Porojnicu Stelian, p. 17; Alberto Loyo, p. 18; William Manning/ Alamy, p. 19; Villiers Steyn, p. 20; Maggy Meyer, p. 21 (African lion); Volodymyr Burdiak, p. 21 (zebra); Thanwan Singh Pannu, p. 21 (giraffe); BlueOrange Studio, p. 21 (savannah grasses); poeticpenguin, p. 21 (spotted hyena); M Rutherford, p. 21 (acacia tree).